CW01086427

SOMERSET & DORSET

Edited By Machaela Gavaghan

First published in Great Britain in 2018 by:

Young Writers
Remus House
Coltsfoot Drive
Peterborough
PE2 9BF
Telephone: 01733 890066
Website: www.youngwriters.co.uk

FOREWORD

Young Writers was created in 1991 with the express purpose of promoting and encouraging creative writing. Each competition we create is tailored to the relevant age group, hopefully giving each child the inspiration and incentive to create their own piece of writing, whether it's a poem or a short story. We truly believe that seeing it in print gives pupils a sense of achievement and pride in their work and themselves.

Our latest competition, Monster Poetry, focuses on uncovering the different techniques used in poetry and encouraging pupils to explore new ways to write a poem. Using a mix of imagination, expression and poetic styles, this anthology is an impressive snapshot of the inventive, original and skilful writing of young people today. These poems showcase the creativity and talent of these budding new writers as they learn the skills of writing, and we hope you are as entertained by them as we are.

CONTENTS

Kadey Paige Sanders (8)	64	Ollie (9)	112
Sam Kirkpatrick (9)	65	Josh Butler (9)	114
Maisey-Rae Olivia McGrath (8)	66	Amelie R (9)	116
Tulysha Gawronska (8)	67	Calum Joyce (9)	118
George Miller (8)	68	Oscar J (9)	120
Cassey Norton (8)	69	Bethany S (9)	122
Serafina Winifred Taylor (9)	70	Aaliyah Samuels (9)	124
Caleb Pack (9)	71	Samuel White (9)	126
Jasper Topliss (8)	72	Fred Parsons (9)	128
Joshua Hudson (9)	73	Aidan U (8)	129
Carmen-Angel Masters O'Brien (9)	74	Travis G (8)	130
Henley Kellaway (7)	75	Leo Xabier Ogilvie-Arregui (9)	132
Kieron Martin (8)	76	Isabelle S (9)	133
Thomas Mepham (9)	77	Jack F (9)	134
Natalie Kate Louise Wilson (9)	78	Summer L (8)	136
Ethan Hayes (9)	79	Daisy Asker (9)	138
Lillianne Tarogi (8)	80	Lily Coltman (9)	139
Bernadette Kaye Champion (8)	81	Neve Docherty (9)	140
Joseph Brown (7)	82	Roman Rain Hardman (9)	141
		Jack M (9)	142
		Rosemary Janet Bradford (8)	143

St Michael's Academy, Grass Royal

Harry Bunkin (7)	83	Bella H (9)	144
Milena Piorkowska (8)	84	Calum R (9)	145
		Ryan L (8)	146

Stourfield Junior School, Bournemouth

		Joel Asher Cohn (9)	147
		Ella Eva Werkentin Chant (9)	148
		Poppy Hannah Blair (9)	149
Isabelle Cotterill (9)	85	Harry Went (9)	150
Ellie Ogden (9)	86	Daisy Fletcher (10)	151
Maya Dixie Hudson (9)	88	Millie Fisher-Wyatt (9)	152
Finian H (9)	90	Evie Millington (9)	153
Julianna T (9)	92	Iris F (8)	154
Elliott W (8)	94	Logan William Goodfellow-Martin (9)	155
Matilda Myers (9)	96	Troy Wilson (9)	156
Poppy Miller (9)	98	Joe Nash (9)	157
Alfie Joshua David Yarwood (9)	100	Harry Illsley (9)	158
Samuel Sydney Price (9)	102	Keira-Anne Erwood (9)	159
Aneta Banyaiova (9)	104	Oliver Knighton (9)	160
Sam Coltman (9)	106	Matthew Dewerenda (9)	161
Ruby Bond (9)	108	Finley Stephen Smithers (9)	162
Alex Shepherd (9)	110	Evan Stoddart-Ceren (9)	163
		Tom C (8)	164

Louise Aravell Calimlim Manabat (8)	165
Lola Bea Whitney (9)	166
Archie Arthur Hamilton (9)	167
Ewan Brooks (9)	168
Charlie Jones (9)	169
Sammy Soltys (9)	170
William Adams (9)	171
Harry Kenyon (9)	172

West Monkton CE Primary School, Taunton

Paddy Hazeldine (10)	173
Reece Fortnum (9)	174
Lewis Ward (10)	176
Jacob Stone (10)	177
Isabella Pereira (10)	178
Imogen Canney (10)	179
Grace Olivia Baker (10)	180
Josie Leanne Corry (9)	181
Cameron Gage (10)	182
Luke Christopher John Rees (10)	183
Kaden Stretton (10)	184
Zuzanna Bukowska (10)	185
Theo Bimson (10)	186
Rosina Coppola (10)	187
Mason James Kew (9)	188
Ruby Wyatt (10)	189
Carys Griffiths-Jones (9)	190
James Metcalfe (10)	191
Kadie Hollins (10)	192
Kobi Loveridge (10)	193

THE POEMS

Grottle Goo

He has fangs like Dracula
His name is Grottle Goo
Sticky and slimy
As clever as anything else
He can climb walls with his sticky pads
Flying like a dragon in the sky
He can change into any shape
His favourite food is a slime pot
He is kind and good at winning battles
Because he is a shape-shifter
Grottle Goo is scary with his bloodthirsty fangs!

Lexi Spencer (9)

Oh Silly Samantha

Samantha was as silly as could be,
She was so clumsy, she would try and stop,
She actually banged heads with a cop!
Samantha was sad, as sad as could be,
"Come here Samantha, come with me."
Samantha came and sat down,
"Boohoo!" Samantha cried,
"No one likes me because I'm clumsy."
Samantha was thinking and then said,
"You know what? I don't think I'm clumsy at all,
I'm going for a lie down in my bed."
"Oh silly Samantha, can't you see?
You're just as fine as can be!"
"Oh yes, yes I am, yes I agree,
I am the best!"
Samantha made new friends,
Do you think there will be another story of Silly
Samantha?
Well, it depends!

Matilda Ruby Male (9)
Bishop Henderson CE Primary School, Taunton

The Tickle Monster

The tickle monster is very funny
The tickle monster has a bunny
The tickle monster smells your tummy
The tickle monster likes your mummy
The tickle monster is silly
The tickle monster is called Billy
The tickle monster drinks honey
The tickle monster likes the word 'bunny'
The tickle monster likes it sunny
The tickle monster is bad
The tickle monster is mad
The tickle monster is sad
The tickle monster has a wife
The tickle monster has a sharp knife
The tickle monster eats logs
The tickle monster hates dogs
The tickle monster lives in bogs
The tickle monster is very ticklish.

Ellena Marie Keeble (8)
Bishop Henderson CE Primary School, Taunton

Alone Cry Eye...

Blue, dripping skin drips down his scaly body as
slow as a snail.
As green as grass, a broccoli head will alert him
when it's time for bed.
Cry Eye will cry and cry
Until his blue skin will die.
He will fake it and ache it,
Then people help him and get poisoned
Like the others and that's what he did with his
brothers!
He will be as quick as lightning
Eating the human body flesh
But when Cry Eye is finished,
He will make such a mess!
Now his broccoli is ringing
And it is time for bed.

Freddie McCarthy (9)
Bishop Henderson CE Primary School, Taunton

Monster, Monster

Monster, monster, show your claws
Monster, monster, has great yawns
Monster, monster is so scary scary
And wants to be hairy
Monster likes pearls
Monster, monster, everyone's scared
Monster, monster, won't play fair
Monster, monster, his name is Tim
Monster, monster, they hate him
Monster, monster, he's very sad
Monser, monster is actually mad!

Alexander James Coles (8)
Bishop Henderson CE Primary School, Taunton

The M-Fair Song

The ocean is my home,
We have lots of fun.
I really miss my mother,
I want her to bake me a bun.

I am a rebel and I know it
So I dyed my fur red.
I did my bit for my herd before
But now I wish them all dead.

I know I am marine life
But I still can live on land
To scare away the boys and girls,
I will never lend a hand.

Emily Wellman (11) & Lilianne
Bishop Henderson CE Primary School, Taunton

Beware, The Nightmare

In the cupboard every night
It stays there waiting for an unlucky soul
That touches him once they open the door.

Beware, beware
The nightmare
The evilness inside
Will crunch you down to the bone
It doesn't care
Even when the humans moan and groan.

Beware, beware
The nightmare.

Daniel Seeley (9)
Bishop Henderson CE Primary School, Taunton

Glimmer's Day

I get up each and every morning,
Still feeling tired and yawny.
I don't wear clothes, my fur is enough,
And I start each morning with sugar puffs.
My day is just beginning,
I've got lots of things planned,
I'm going to help some children out,
Can you give me a hand?

When I get there,
They're playing and messing about,
I let out a massive roar.
That surprised them, that's for sure!
They begin to listen to what I say,
From now on, I can let them play.
The next thing they learn to do
Is a lesson on how to tie their shoe.
Suddenly, the bell goes for lunch,
All I hear is *munch, munch, munch!*
When they are back for lessons,
It is time for art,
We make some big behaviour charts.

After the lesson is over,
We spot a three-leafed clover.
When it is time to go,
The children start to moan
Because they don't want to go home.

When I get to my house,
I have my dinner, which is pickled mouse.
When I go to bed,
I start dreaming in my head.

Maisie Cadwallader (9)

Hayeswood First School, Colehill

Patch

This is a poem about my best friend Patch,
He came to Earth one day in a spaceship with a hatch.
Patch came from Jupiter, a planet far away,
He landed in my back garden, ready for us to play.
His hair was the colour of a Galaxy with silver gems on it.
If you looked into his eyes, you'd be hypnotised for a bit.
He talked about his friends, Bubbles and the triplets Zig, Zog and Zag.
We played games in the garden, his favourite was tag.
Then we went to a museum to learn about Earth's history.
My favourite display was the Pyramids
so Patch told me the mystery
Of how his grandad built the Pyramids a long time ago.
We chatted about it for hours until it was time to go.

Next we went to the beach,
It was sunny with a light breeze.
I bought Patch an ice cream and he got brain freeze!
The sun started setting, it was time to say goodbye.
We walked back to my garden and I tried not to cry.
Patch climbed into his spaceship, ready to fly away.
We had such a good time, maybe he'll visit me again one day.

Trinity Cooper (8)
Hayeswood First School, Colehill

Buck And His Brilliant Monsters

The monsters live in Monsterville,
To get there, you have to go over a very big hill.
The monsters there are all shapes and sizes,
Some are tall, some are small,
Some bounce like a ball.
A monster's name was Buck,
He had very good luck.
The monster had lots of friends,
But this is not where our story ends.

Football is his favourite sport,
He dreams to beat the town's team one day.
"Here's the trophy Buck, take it away,"
That's what he hopes the ref will say.
The big chance came one Saturday,
The monsters gathered around a football player recruiting poster.
One even dropped his coffee from Costa.
Buck gathered his team, they packed their kits,
So excited to be playing on a real pitch.

Buck and his brilliant monsters,
That afternoon, Buck's dreams came true,
As his team won by two.
Just as Buck dreamt it would be,
The referee handed him the trophy,
And he beamed with glee!

Harrison Larcombe (9)
Hayeswood First School, Colehill

Blood Demon

Blood Demon was created by toxic waste,
Seeping right down to the depths of Hell.
His only friends were terror and food,
Which he must search for in the world above.

He moves in a swift, sneakily way,
His eyes are the colour of a new blood moon.
Seeking, searching, squinting for some snacks
With a wicked grin spread across his foul face.

When they felt the presence of him,
The trees gave way like a crowd parting for a king.
He had tried his hardest to be kind
But even the toughest animals ran away.

His stomach made an epic rumble,
As loud as thunder in a storm.
A small child walking by heard the rumble
And she found him and shared some food.
"Oh, thanks!" he boomed with massive joy,

"Hang on a sec, why aren't you scared?"
"You looked ever so hungry so I tried to help."

And that's how Alice and Blood Demon made friends.

Jakob Bennett (8)
Hayeswood First School, Colehill

Fear Papallymus!

My name is Papallymus
I lurk in my dim palace.
It is cavernous and dark
Like the depths of my heart!
My skin is black like the void
The green spots on my flesh you want to avoid.
My razor-sharp claws will rip you to shreds
But you won't be as tasty as my favourite -
frogs' legs!
I have the horns of the Devil
And luminous, orange eyes,
Which you don't want to meddle.
I have foul-smelling breath
With rotten, yellow teeth,
All these three things create much more mischief!
I leave my underground palace in the gloomy night
And when people see me,
They will scream with fright.
"He has seen us, he has seen us!
Fear Papallymus!"

Phoebe Powell (9)
Hayeswood First School, Colehill

Who's Under Your Bed?

Have you ever wondered who is the one
Messing up your plans like going for a run?
Things that you put down are no longer there
When he jumps up behind you and gives you a big
scare.
Massive wings, raging teeth, unicorn horn and
beady eyes.
Is he there? No, he's not.
With his powers fit for spies,
His invisible cloak surrounds him like a vampire at
midnight.
Is he flying a kite?
You'll never know for in the night,
He'll give you such a fright.
Tuck yourself in, read a book, cuddle your ted
And turn off your light, brush your teeth,
Ready for the night.
Before you go to sleep,
Check under your bed for you may see Wahoo
Biggelsworth!

Lily Edwards (9)
Hayeswood First School, Colehill

Blobby's Adventure!

Blobby the blob lives beneath the sand,
He wants to explore every part of the land.
With his violet fur and pink patches,
He likes to eat whatever he catches.
Whatever he sees, he can't ignore,
However, people can't hear him snore.
He'd like to visit wonderful Spain,
Do you think he'd like to fly on a plane?
He has one friend who lives next door
But in Spain, he thinks he might find some more.
Let's wish Blobby luck
On the adventure of his life,
I really, really hope he finds a nice wife.

Honor Mae Barfoot (8)
Hayeswood First School, Colehill

Midnight Monsters

Little creatures crawl across your floor,
You'll never know when they'll open your door.
They tiptoe around the house at night,
Beware, they might give you a fright.

They like to nibble upon your toes,
So keep them tucked inside your clothes.
You could offer them crumbs as a treat
To stop them munching at your feet.

Little monsters love to play
So make sure you put your toys away.
I think monster babes are sweet
With their waving hands and fluffy feet.

Jemima Turner (9)
Hayeswood First School, Colehill

Who's That Hiding Under Your Bed?

Who's hiding under your bed at night?
Who gives you an awful fright?
Who eats all your cake?
Who makes you shake?
What can you hear if you lay very still?
It looks scary like Cruella de Vil,
What is that creeping around your room?
Maybe it is the dreadful doom!
Shadows on your wall,
The monster looks very tall.
My iPad is there on the ground,
Listen, what's that sound?
The monster is creeping towards my iPad,
Shall I call my dad?

Isobel Pinto (9)
Hayeswood First School, Colehill

Scribbles' Life

Scribbles is a young monster
Who likes to mess around
If you wanted to adopt her
She'd probably cost more than a pound
She has pearly-white fangs
That appear when she smiles
She has bright blue, fluffy hair
That she swishes like she just doesn't care!
If you head over to the roller coasters
You'll find her there
Candyfloss is her number one food
Especially when she is in a good mood.

Scarlett Seagrove (9)
Hayeswood First School, Colehill

Monty The Monstersaurus

A big, fat, friendly monster came to school with me today.
I didn't want my teachers to see so I hid him right away.
I put him in the cupboard with all the books
But he went into the dinner hall and frightened the cooks!
He said, "My name is Monty,
I'm friendly, don't you know?
I'll see you all another day
because now I've got to go!"

Ruby Whittle (8)
Hayeswood First School, Colehill

My Monster

I think there is a monster under my bed
But it's probably just in my head
Monster, monster, please come out
Monster, monster, stop hanging about
When I am in a deep, dreamy sleep
My monster keeps on counting sheep
It keeps my nightmares away
And so I think I'll let it stay
My monster is not scary
It is just hairy.

Rebecca Gillard (8)
Hayeswood First School, Colehill

The Little Monster

She comes from Mars,
Her favourite food is chocolate bars.
She's a good little monster
But be careful, she can be quite a trickster!
She's got a friend that's greedy
And to burn off some energy, she has to be very
speedy.
When Scarlett goes to bed, she's as snug as a bug
And then I give her a big goodnight hug.

Grace Gallienne (9)
Hayeswood First School, Colehill

Shortasaurus And His Many Legs

My name is Shortasaurus
I have lots and lots of legs
Watch out for my laser beams
They will cut you into shreds
I am brilliant at shape-shifting
You will never see me go
And with my spots to hide
And antennae to see
I keep myself low.

Ewan Trimmer (8)
Hayeswood First School, Colehill

The Worry Monster

Teeth are sharp as daggers
Eyes as deep as the ocean
When I worry, he rears his ugly head
He can be found under my bed
When I see him, I'm as brave as can be
I send him love and invite him for tea.

Oliver Quirk (8)

Hayeswood First School, Colehill

Shape-Shifter

I was born on the mountains way up high
I've got green skin like grass
Run down the mountains
You won't see me
A shape-shifter
I will be.

Kacey Esposito (9)
Hayeswood First School, Colehill

Terror

With long, green legs
Big, black eyes
Huge, red horns
Giant, carrot-like fangs
That is Terror.

James Cheese (9)
Hayeswood First School, Colehill

Target

(A haiku)

His horn is blood-red
Eyes yellower than the sun
Target-like body.

Rowan Barr (9)

Hayeswood First School, Colehill

The Adventure With Guppy

I have this little monster all fluffy and pink
She loves to rule the universe,
Well, that's what I think.
She goes around town and loves to chat
But then I have a frown and she comes back.
"What is wrong?"
I say, "It's Scrummy Scrum!"
She has a frown.
"I feel the sadness little Gup
But why don't we go to Scrummy Scrum?"
I say, "Oh boy oh boy, when do we go?"
So we head to Scrummy Scrum.
"What about now?"
Then I say, "Wow!"
After I say, "Pow!"
"Who are your friends?"
Guppy says, "They're Poppy, Sloppy, Toppy and
Moppy."

We see butterflies and bees,
We have to find the crystal
But then Guppy says, "I've got a thistle!"

We don't find the crystal,
We have lunch with the Queen,
Darts, parts and scarves for Guppy!

Megan Bird (9)
Ilchester Community School (Junior), Ilchester

Fang's Plan To Destroy The Supermarket

One day I went to the supermarket
And I met a monster
Who was as scary as a dragon.
I said hi, he said nothing,
He was a mean monster.
Then another mean monster called Killer came,
"I'm as hot as the sun!" said Killer.
"So am I," said Fang.
"I'm as cold as a freezing iceberg!" I said.
Killer's head was ruby-red,
We were about a mile away from the supermarket
When *boom!* The supermarket blew into shreds.
"Yes, our plan worked!" said Killer and Fang
As they ran as fast as cheetahs.
"Come back here!" said the shopkeeper
As he tried to run as fast as a cheetah.
"What a weird day," I said
As I sat down on my sofa as slow as a snail.

Dallan John Murphy (8)

Ilchester Community School (Junior), Ilchester

The Super Monster

I saw a cute, cuddly, fluffy monster
Covered in beautiful colours, red and blue
Unfortunately, he didn't have a friend
And he was three foot two.

When I saw him, he told me he had a den
It was quite unusual
His house was number 10
We went for a walk and came across a school
He saw a lot of people
Chucking and throwing balls like an Olympian
He heard a loud scream
So went to find out without a doubt
He saw an evil monster run inside like steam
He looked in a class, then looked in a cupboard
He went in, he saw a rubber
It was grey, green and black
So we shut the door and locked it up
Now everyone and everything is back.

Sonny Girling (9)
Ilchester Community School (Junior), Ilchester

Fuzzy Buzzy Goes To The Shop

One day Miss Fuzzy Buzzy went to the shop,
She went into the shop and did a big hop.
In the shop, she bought a pot,
In the sun, it was quite hot.
People thought she was mean
But she was kind, friendly, helpful like me.
People thought she was a he
Because of the way she did a wee.
She felt embarrassed about the way she weed,
She tripped over her pot and saw a trampoline.
She jumped up and hopped over,
She did a hop and a skip
And twizzled around like a Jelly Tot.
She did a big hop,
She fell onto the floor
But did not appear.
She ended up at the end of the shop!

Grace Caroline Beard (9)

Ilchester Community School (Junior), Ilchester

The Day With My Monster

I saw a red, short, gentle creature
All short and cute, it was about two foot one
It did no harm and it wasn't a pet
I took her to school
Small enough to fit in my bag
She's slow to move like a tortoise
A heart as warm as fire
Nothing to stop her glowing in the sun
People love her like a pet
It does not matter what she is
People love her as a child
With one hundred teeth in one mouth
When she's sad, she's as blue as the ocean
When she's hungry, we have fish and chips
All warm and nice
Home to have a nice rest
A small bed next to mine.

Amanda Plunkett (9)

Ilchester Community School (Junior), Ilchester

Under The Sea

I went under the sea with Karnkey
And found a cave and found treasure
We heard bones rattling like knives and forks
And saw skeleton pirates
Smelt revolting, rotting flesh
Opened the chest, gold and silver
With beautiful coloured gems
Blue, orange, red, yellow
Floating back up to the surface
A shark was chasing us
We swam as fast as we could
But started to sink down deep
I kicked my legs to float back up
I found myself in danger
Karnkey swam in and saved me
That day was absolutely amazing
I will go on an adventure again
With my best friend.

Finley du Feu (8)
Ilchester Community School (Junior), Ilchester

The Flein

The monster Spiky lived in Monster University,
Spiky had ten friends who were monsters
But one of them was a human.
Everyone thought it was a girl
But he was a boy and still my best friend forever,
Spiky always visited me at school.

Spiky went to school,
He thought pencils were toothbrushes
And all that stuff.
Spiky was as fluffy as me,
He went to the shop
And bought a hotpot.
My monster thought school was cool
And when the monster went to the children,
They cried and wanted him to be fried.
He died so he can never visit me ever, ever again.

Isabelle Grace Ferguson (8)
Ilchester Community School (Junior), Ilchester

My Invisible Monster

Once I went to Raccoon Land
And I felt something rather strange
It was a monster
But he was as fuzzy as a cat
I asked him if he wanted to come to Planet Earth
"Of course I will," he said
I told him the directions
And he flew me home in his spaceship
I think he had a crush on me
I was really rather red
But where had he gone?
I thought he'd run away from me
"Bye-bye monster, I'll see you soon."
But what was happening to me?
I was turning invisible you see,
"Bye-bye monster, if you're running away from
me."

Jamie Goodall (8)
Ilchester Community School (Junior), Ilchester

The Crazy Monster

On the way to the moon
I heard a great big roar like thunder
I landed on another planet
That was pink and blue
I saw the beast
From the east
He had his eye on me
Looking for a feast
Then he ran like the wind
He told me his plan to take over the world
I was very upset
"I don't want to help you take over the world."
Then the monster wanted to do a floss challenge
But the monster won
He loved candy so I gave the monster some candy.
The next day he was going to take over the world
But I ran to my rocket
And blasted off.

Noah Hughes (8)
Ilchester Community School (Junior), Ilchester

A Monster's Day At School

On the way to school,
I met a pink, furry, cute monster.
She told me her name was Bubblegum
And that her favourite food was Haribo.
So I took her to school and here is what she did.
She pricked Peter the art teacher,
Hurt Herminoy the English teacher
And at lunchtime,
She threw the food across the hall
And it landed on the lunch man, Paul!
She stuffed the pudding in my face
And ran across the hall in a pace,
Then ran from the school and I couldn't find her,
I hoped she would come again some time
But I never saw her again.

Ava Reason (8)
Ilchester Community School (Junior), Ilchester

Mr Fluffy-Pluffy's First Day To Drive A Car

The monster Fluffy-Pluffy was born in the town
called Monster Imagine Land.
My monster is a bit good and sometimes he is
crazy.
Me and Fluffy-Pluffy are friends,
Our friendship will never end.
We woke up and we saw it was late for school.
We went downstairs ready for school
But the car was not so cool.

At school, the children cried
And the teachers sighed.
After we put things to prepare,
We tried to drive but the people wanted to stare.
Fluffy-Pluffy got more things for the car from the
shops
and came back to hide from the cops.

Gaia Errico (9)
Ilchester Community School (Junior), Ilchester

Fluffy's Day At School

On the way to school, I saw a big blob.
It looked orangey-green, not very scary,
I peered through the bush,
When I walked past it, it followed me.
It was orange like an orange
But it was fluffy, which was weird.
I said, "Come with me to school."
It jumped like a jumping jack.

When we got there,
He crashed and smacked.
I went to see what it was,
He was crashing into stuff like a ball!

When we got home,
I said, "Good boy."
I hope he will come back for dinner sometime.

Amelia Isabella Pagano (8)
Ilchester Community School (Junior), Ilchester

Fuzmo Saving The World

When I saw a lost, lonely monster
In the Monster Inc cinema,
I felt as scared as a boy seeing a monster.
He explained how his best friend, the Devil,
Was ruby-red and liked killing the town.
His colour was as bright as the sun
And it burnt my eye.
He heard a big bang and his big, bright necklace shined.
He said, "It is time for me to go."
He skated away on his skateboard,
He trapped the Devil in a mine.
The marvellous mine avalanched down
And the deadly Devil was no more.

Alyssa Heddon (9)

Ilchester Community School (Junior), Ilchester

Blood Ripper

Blood Ripper was born in a place
Cloud City was its name
It needed to be scary
So to the beach it came
I met him on the beach
I saw his hypnotising eye
When the people saw him
They all said goodbye
I needed to be brave
So I didn't run away
But if I failed this
I could be in a grave
He had fangs shorter than knives
And the same with his nails
He had dark green skin and magnificent wings
He also had six horns coming out of his head
Then I knew I was dead.

Dexter Michael Henry (9)
Ilchester Community School (Junior), Ilchester

The Football Match

L ickertung is my best friend.

I t was the day of the football match.

"C orn is the best foot for football," said Lickertung.

K ick-off went to the other team.

E verybody was happy and Lickertung was going to scream because Blood Reaper was on the team.

R unning was all we needed.

T he crowd were going wild.

U ncle Troll came on the team.

N othing got in our way.

G oal! We scored a goal and then we won. I was so happy!

Luke Babb (8)
Ilchester Community School (Junior), Ilchester

A Day At The Park

There once lived a monster called Skinny
And he lived underground.
When he was digging,
He saw some metal.
The colour was red
So skinny dug it up.
Skinny the monster heard a noise,
It was a little girl on the swings.
The little girl was called Kate,
She was a nice girl.
She was pretty like blooming flowers,
Her hair was blonde and she had a daisy in her
hair.
Skinny had three hats and mats on him,
The mat was in a ball like some hats that had pom-
poms on them.

Evie Baul (8)
Ilchester Community School (Junior), Ilchester

Cute Fluffkins And Me

Cute Fluffkins lives under my bed,
We got up and went to Amazing Amusements.
We spent all our 2ps,
We could smell sweet sweets.
We could hear money rattling like keys being
dropped.
We could feel the beautiful breeze coming in from
the doors.
We could see machines with buttons everywhere.
Me and my monster saw one of our friends,
We have lots of lovely friends,
Me and my monster are very nice to each other.
At home, we had all of our candyfloss,
It was so sweet.

Olivia Horne (8)
Ilchester Community School (Junior), Ilchester

A Day With Skates-Kates And The Queen!

Skates-Kates loved to rapidly roll to the park,
Windy weather rolled her down the bumpy hill.
Razor-sharp teeth chattered through the breeze of winter.
I span the roundabout faster and faster,
I stood in the queue and some guards like you
Seen on the TV, surrounding the Queen.
"She must be important."
"Oh yes, she is the Queen!" Skates-Kates gasped.
We ate lunch, such a glorious lunch!
"I hope I see you again!" she said.

Sophie Rogers (8)
Ilchester Community School (Junior), Ilchester

Gut Ripper's Evil Plan

The gross Gut Ripper is tough and disgusting
We go to the sea, where he has a big pee
He wears a special suit so he can't get harmed
He drops a toxic bomb
No one knows where it's come from
He is like a green ghost
Which has taken over the coast
He dissolves everything except me
Soon he wants to get me
I set it alight and stand next to it
He comes charging and falls right in
"I'm sorry," he splutters as he sinks away.

Lincoln James Regan (9)
Ilchester Community School (Junior), Ilchester

The Slime From Hell!

One day I heard a massive roar
And a weird splodging sound.
A slime monster from Hell appeared,
Oh my goodness, what had I found?
The portal he came from led to Hell,
He had teeth all around his mouth that rotated!
He had some spikes on his head,
Which helped him in battle.
I could see he was literally made of slime
And he had four arms dripping with slime!
As soon as I saw this monstrous beast,
I smiled with my sharp, rotating teeth!

Shaun Thomas Mayou (9)
Ilchester Community School (Junior), Ilchester

Scratch's Day At The Park

Once there was a monster called Scratch,
He was born in a volcano.
His eyes glowed like the sun.
When I met him, he looked terrifying
But when I looked at him again,
I saw he was scared.
Soon, I took him to the park
And everybody was scared of him
But really, he was really kind.
Soon, me and Scratch went on all the equipment in
the colossal park.
Soon, we got tired and started heading home
And I took care of him with all of my heart.

Dylan Tomos Edwards (8)

Ilchester Community School (Junior), Ilchester

Loral And Oliver

I saw two monsters named Loral and Oliver.
Two weeks later I saw
Loral and Oliver fighting
Loral scratched Oliver and
They were no longer friends.
Loral came to my house
And slept under my bed,
She met Oliver there.
Loral and Oliver got back together
And fell in love forever!

One day a griffin came.
He was after Oliver and Loral,
So I pulled Loral and Oliver and took care of them.
The griffin never came back again.

Kira MacIntyre (8)
Ilchester Community School (Junior), Ilchester

A Trip To The Park With Conner

I met Conner whilst going home from school,
He was sitting on a stool.
When we got home,
He ate the phone.
"Oh no!" yelled Mum,
"Give me some gum!"
But I took him to the park,
He bit a swing, which gave him a ting.
He cracked the crooked climbing frame,
Then played a game.
He scrapped the slow see-saw,
Though now, he was feeling very poor
So he left the poor park
When it was finally getting dark.

Jack Ethan Tucker (9)
Ilchester Community School (Junior), Ilchester

The Day My Monster Came To School

My monster nibbled my pencil,
My monster ripped my book.
My monster even ate a chair,
My monster got a stare.
My monster ate the children's bags in one big munch.
My monster ate the children's lunch!
My monster ate all the coats up,
My monster even broke a cup!
My monster got another stare,
My monster was new to this planet.
My monster needed some time,
My monster needed some time to learn, now it's your turn!

Georgia-Mae Olivia Carey (7)
Ilchester Community School (Junior), Ilchester

The Demon Eye

Once, there was a monster called Demon Eye,
He lived in an abandoned mine,
It was as dark as night in the deep mine.
One day, the monster went to a supermarket,
He made the biggest mess in the universe!
His skin was ruby-red,
When he went to the seaside,
I made a hole in the sand
And trapped Demon Eye.
When the water came in,
His skin sizzled in the trap.
"I am sorry," he said
And then he turned to stone.

Archie William Camm (9)
Ilchester Community School (Junior), Ilchester

My Slimy Adventure With Wobby

I saw a blinding, bright blob
Slowly slithering like a tired snake
I asked where it was from
She said she was from the moon
The monster took me to her home
All I could see were spaceships
And all I could hear was the monsters eating
Gobble, gobble!
I could smell other aliens
Being cooked over an open fire
I could feel the dazzling dust of the moon
Wobby gave me some odd food
It did not taste nice!

Ruby Louise Sutton (9)
Ilchester Community School (Junior), Ilchester

Cuddly

There once was a monster called Cuddly
And he lived on a planet called Pluto.
He lived in a can but then he got banned.
I was on my way out of school when I saw him.
I said, "Hi."
But he said, "Bye."

Later we met each other on the beach
And we both said, "Hi!"
And when it was lunch,
We had brunch.
He asked, "Want to go?"
I said, "Hey, marvellous monster!"

Reece Davies (9)
Ilchester Community School (Junior), Ilchester

The Day Flubber Bogey Went To The Shops

Once there lived a monster called The Flubber
Bogey.
I met him under my bed just when my head hit his.
Mum gave me a call to go to the supermarket,
I knew I couldn't have him so I hid him in my
jumper.

When we got there, he snuck in the pick and mix
aisle.
He ended up in a pile of fizzy swirls!
When he got out, he ended up in curls
But my mum saw and shut him in a door
And he was no more than a blob of slime!

Aoife Mordue (8)
Ilchester Community School (Junior), Ilchester

58

My Marvellous Monster

I was staring out of the window,
Almost zoning out,
But just then, I saw an orange thing
Drop down onto the roundabout.
When I took him out is when he got naughty,
Moggy said all about his old pals.
One is called Porty, Corty and one more named
Snorty.

The next morning he carried my bed
Onto a starship and flew to Bobble Planet.
They have a food called Snow Berries
But on Earth, they have banned it.

Rebecca Jane Johnson (9)
Ilchester Community School (Junior), Ilchester

The Day Out

On the way to town,
I met a fluffy monster
With a cute face and fluffy skin.
His skin was orange,
Unfortunately, he didn't have any friends
So we took him in the car.
He was about six foot two,
We took him to the shop.
He picked out some clothes,
We got some delicious, scrumptious lunch.
We heard birds squawking,
We smelt pizza.
We felt soft, soothing blankets,
We tasted pizza.

Aimee Simpson (8)
Ilchester Community School (Junior), Ilchester

Evil To Friendly

M agnificent monster
O n the sea with some of me
N aughty but friendly, cool like me
S illy, stinky
T errifying before but friendly now
E very day he sleeps until noon
R acing and leaking, sometimes shaking.

G reat with a cat
L onely and bony
O ver the moon
O verjoyed
C razy and lazy
H appy and slappy.

Austin Searle (7)
Ilchester Community School (Junior), Ilchester

The Monster From Heaven

The dragon snake was born in a cave
It has six friends and it is very good.
One day he left the cave
I met the dragon snake at the beach
It took me to its birthplace
It was in Scandinavia
We played tag and fetch
He rode at speed around the world
He put me to bed then flew away
He went to see his monster friends.
I can still hear his roar
I can still smell his flames as well.

Jasper Lilly (8)
Ilchester Community School (Junior), Ilchester

The Monster Named Fuzzball Who Went To School

Once there was a monster named Fuzzball
Who liked to play football.
At 12 o'clock, it had lunch,
Then had a munch, munch, munch!

When school finished, he got ice cream,
Then he got home, he had some bread
And then he went straight to bed.
He met a monster named Chad
And he liked to be bad.
When he went to school,
Someone called him a fool.

Leo Rahman (8)
Ilchester Community School (Junior), Ilchester

Fuzzball At School!

Fuzzball was at home feeling lonely
Because no one liked him at all.
He stayed at home just reading
Until someone invited him to the school pool!
He was so excited, he'd never been so excited before!
He flew down as fast as he could.
When he got there, it was like he was in a desert!
When he asked to fly a kite,
The teacher said, "Of course!"

Kadey Paige Sanders (8)
Ilchester Community School (Junior), Ilchester

The Devil's Brother Takes Over The Earth

There once was a devil whose mum was an angel
And his dad was the Devil.
When the Devil was born,
It had an evil plan to take over Earth,
It lived in Hell.
When it was older, it went to Earth and killed
everyone.
It went back to Hell,
As he was getting lifted back up,
He saw an amazing view
And thought to himself, *what a beautiful world!*

Sam Kirkpatrick (9)
Ilchester Community School (Junior), Ilchester

School Trip

I was walking to school on a summer's day
When I saw a friendly monster
His name was Harry
We went to school
My teacher was happy, she loved monsters
She said, "Do you want to come to the ice cream
shop?"
Harry said, "Yes!"
On the bus they went
To get their treats
Ice as cold as the Arctic
But delicious to taste.

Maisey-Rae Olivia McGrath (8)
Ilchester Community School (Junior), Ilchester

66

Mr Hornery's First Time At Killer School

Mr Hornery goes to Killer School,
The teacher said, "Let's sneak outside
And I will kill that deer that tastes like beer."
Mr Hornery tried but he did it all wrong.
At school, Mr Hornery cried,
Then the teacher sighed
And guided him to the room.
Boom, the door went,
He had to kill a frog
That looked like a dog.

Tulysha Gawronska (8)
Ilchester Community School (Junior), Ilchester

Mr Max

One day Mr Max went to school
And he went to teach marvellous maths
After school he went to the shops
He bought some monster food
He drove home in his red and gold lamborghini
He started to cook some terrifying tea
Then Mr Max stomped to the park
Then he went to buy some tickets
So he could watch the Monster Mash-up match.

George Miller (8)
Ilchester Community School (Junior), Ilchester

The School Monster

On the way to school,
I met a monster all fluffy and peach.
It wasn't a little lost pet
Or a huge lost pet.
She was about seven foot two,
Her teeth were fangs,
Yet she was a friendly creature.
She was a little weird,
When I asked to play ball
"Of course," said she,
We ran around like mad!

Cassey Norton (8)
Ilchester Community School (Junior), Ilchester

Knife Killers

In search for a monster
Guided by sweet humming
As I got closer, I saw two mysterious monsters
Both had crooked teeth, one had eyes with a soul
Heartbreaking to look at
Ears like shining pieces of the sun
I approached this beast
And it smiled at me
It was breathtaking to look
But I smiled back.

Serafina Winifred Taylor (9)
Ilchester Community School (Junior), Ilchester

Ziggy At School

Ziggy was walking through the park
Until a boy so friendly came over
And picked him up in the dark
And stayed in his room,
Where he felt like doom.
He took him to school
But he didn't have friends
Because they thought he was cruel.
They thought he was a rickety, old creature!

Caleb Pack (9)
Ilchester Community School (Junior), Ilchester

The Great Adventure

I saw a creature hovering above the bushes
Like a menacing wasp
Dashing and darting, dipping and diving
Hurling me onto his back, we were off
Grumpily groaning from his jaws
In the distance, I saw a vast volcano
Lava bubbling like a Jacuzzi
The air smelt like burning flesh.

Jasper Topliss (8)
Ilchester Community School (Junior), Ilchester

Living In The Darkness Realm

The Devil was from the Darkness Realm
He went to the office to see who was there
Someone was there, they said,
"Hi, my name is Steve
And I'm going to be your friend forever!"
And it cooed and cooed,
Everyone heard it
And headed out of the Darkness Realm.

Joshua Hudson (9)
Ilchester Community School (Junior), Ilchester

Camo's Revenge

Oen day, when I was in the shop,
I met a monstrous thing.
He ran on his centipede legs
And with his body, he could cling.

He was cross with people,
They cornered and rejected him,
That's why he wanted revenge,
"You make my life so dim!"

Carmen-Angel Masters O'Brien (9)
Ilchester Community School (Junior), Ilchester

Henry And Rale The Universe

Henry the dangerous, deadly monster greeted me
Slimy like a rotten egg
As smelly as ash
Radiating heat like a sizzling bonfire
Living in a vast volcano
Surrounded by lava creatures
Planning to take over the world.

Henley Kellaway (7)

Ilchester Community School (Junior), Ilchester

The Amazing Gloopp

G ood Gloopp is here,

L et's have a party with Gloopp near.

O h, he's so spiky!

O h, he's so slimy!

P ong is the only word he says,

P hooey, he stinks, oh my days!

Kieron Martin (8)

Ilchester Community School (Junior), Ilchester

The Amazing Fluffy

F luffy is there,

L et's have a party.

U h-oh, he's so fluffy,

F luffy is so short.

F luffy is so spiky, his ears are not on him,

Y ou should have him as your pet!

Thomas Mepham (9)

Ilchester Community School (Junior), Ilchester

A Day At The Shop

I was driving to the shop
And I heard a little pop
I opened the door
And then I saw a jiggle
It was Mrs Wiggle
She was happy like jelly
Her belly was like a penny
I ran to her and she ran to me.

Natalie Kate Louise Wilson (9)
Ilchester Community School (Junior), Ilchester

Mr Boloboly Goes To School

S cary monster goes to school,

"C ool, cool, cool!"

H e said.

O n the bus, he banged his head,

O n the bus, he took a selfie,

"L ook at me! He, he."

Ethan Hayes (9)

Ilchester Community School (Junior), Ilchester

Puffy And Me

One day, we played in the park
His hair is brown like chocolate
And his body is fluffy like a teddy bear
He gave me a frightful scare
Everybody was scared
And went to the ice cream truck.

Lillianne Tarogi (8)
Ilchester Community School (Junior), Ilchester

Snowy Day

M easly, shiny

O verjoyed, lovely

N aughty, cheeky

S hort, gentle

T remendous dreamer

E yes as deep as the forest

R osy-red cheeks.

Bernadette Kaye Champion (8)

Ilchester Community School (Junior), Ilchester

The Bigfoot

Strolling on the beach,
A terrible monster I saw.
Nine eyes stared at me,
One sword pointed at me,
I had to be brave!

Joseph Brown (7)
Ilchester Community School (Junior), Ilchester

Pooky The Monster

My name is Pooky
I like to eat a cookie
I saw a cat
It sat on my bedroom mat
I went to look at cars
I have an owner called Lars
It's time for me to have lunch
I will eat bananas in a bunch
I need to pack
I have a big rucksack
See you soon
I will be on the moon.

Harry Bunkin (7)
St Michael's Academy, Grass Royal

What Am I?

My fur is fluffy,
I have a smooth tail.
I have wings but I'm not an angel.
If you stroke me, I will be your pet.
If you distract my slumber, I will tear you to shreds.
What am I?

Milena Piorkowska (8)
St Michael's Academy, Grass Royal

The Grim

The Grim was created in a starless cave,
It had a rocket-propelled horn as sharp as needles.
It searched for helpless unicorns to enslave,
Eyes as dark as the midnight sky.

It departed its residence as nimble as a squirrel,
Ears pricked for powerless unicorns.
Hunting on the rocks, caves and even the beach,
Alarming screams didn't stop it from disappearing.

The Grim eventually reached the misty mountains,
Where his stomach was roaring louder than ever.
Lightning struck his gloomy past,
Right before his eyes,
And it washed the rest goodbye.

And now the cave lies abandoned and gloomy
With no evil cackle to be heard.
Instead, up towards the candy clouds,
Show patches of cheerful sunlight,
Showing where it has been.

Isabelle Cotterill (9)
Stourfield Junior School, Bournemouth

The Heart Collector

The heart collector was born in 1984,
A swirling, whistling whip of wind
Sent the lights in the city dim.
As horrid as the Devil,
A horrifying, ignorant soul,
He is like the darkest shadow.

You know when he's around
But he hardly makes a sound.
The lightest sky turns dark
And you think everything will fall apart.

He collects up souls and hearts like you collect
money.
He takes your life,
He sucks your soul and chucks it out of his window
And keeps the hearts with broken parts.

But one day it all slows down,
He looks at the abandoned, treacherous town,
Sees the damage he has made
And knows it's only him to blame.

He sees bodies on the ground
And is silenced and he doesn't make a sound.

Feeling disheartened inside,
A little girl sees the lonely foe
And comes up beside him.
She looks at him with a friendly, joyful, happy
smile.
Meanwhile, she gets in touch
With his heartless soul
And makes him the kindest fellow.

He is now tranquil, benign and kind in soul,
He is a lovely fellow.
Suddenly a whip of wind starts to carry him away,
He waves bye-bye to a now joyful town
And sheds a tear of memory as he starts to
dissolve on the deep, sky-blue sea.

As he turns into thin air,
His memories will still be shared
Of his kindness and how he cared.

Ellie Ogden (9)
Stourfield Junior School, Bournemouth

The Putrid

There is a miniature monster
Who exists on top of my house.
He has enormous, bulbous eyes
And fur like a mouse.
His body is muddy, rotten and peeling,
Which fell onto the selfish ceiling.

His hair is orange and lime green
With no love hearts to be seen.
While his nose is a brown, funny colour
And his mouth is unearthed in dust,
And when you stare at his back,
He really is a rust.
With sharp, laser fangs
And long, gory hairs,
This creature is sure to be the most disturbing in all
the land.

He left his habitat as quick as a click,
While looking for prey to hunt
And once he'd left his dwelling,
He finally found his livid grunt.

The putrid beast reached the busy beach,
Where his wrath seemed to depart him.
But when he stepped on the soft sand,
Something weird transpired to his brown, mouldy
skin.

He gazed at his feet,
Which looked like a giant marshmallow,
But when he studied closer,
They were turning a bright sun yellow.
His fangs seemed to sink
And his hairs went all pink.
His eyes changed colour to blue and green
And a jungle of hairs like nobody had ever seen.

And now some years have passed,
They have been terrifying.
But over the sand lie jolly footprints,
Showing where this creature has been.

Maya Dixie Hudson (9)
Stourfield Junior School, Bournemouth

Leaf Lover

In the noisy forest was a monster called Leaf
Lover.
The mysterious animal always would guide lost
hikers and give fantastic tours.
He was famous throughout the world.

His face was emerald and soft,
And his body was smooth, brown bark.
He had a colourful flower for his heart
And leaf hair, with white fluffy teeth
That looked like clouds.

One day he left his dwelling to have a vast,
adventurous walk.
He crossed the crystal-clear lakes and snowy
mountains.
The gentleman past villages
And sometimes had tiny breaks
But he never turned back.

At one stop, he missed a sign,
It read in bold writing:

Ahead toxic pond!
The further he trod more of the mud, less shiny
trees.

The monster was about to jog back
But then he flew back into a toxic pool!
His skin sizzled and scorched
And his heart changed into a skull of dread and
pain.
The fiend swam out with poisonous skin
And furious eyes thinking of people's demise.

Now the forest lies dead and full of lice and mice
And no life is settled, except screams and cries.

Finian H (9)
Stourfield Junior School, Bournemouth

The Monster Under My Bed

Once, a monster lived under my bed,
Where no light was able to reach him.
He had demonic eyes filled with fury and hatred
And a jungle of jet-black fur.
He had teeth as sharp as shards of glass
And a crooked unibrow.

The monster crept out from under the bed whilst I
was fast asleep.
A hungry grunt beside my bed nearly woke my
brother up!
Snores still echoed through my room,
I was entranced in my deep sleep.
Suddenly, the monster's stomach gurgled viciously.

Confused, I woke up.
Petrified, I looked around
But my room was very dark.
Cautiously, I turned on the light
And saw the ugly monster.
I froze in fright
And stared at the sight in front of me.

Seconds later, the light washed over him
And his temper seemed to seep away.
His black, matted hair was replaced
With bright yellow fur as soft as sand.
His grey, shallow eyes were replaced
With lime ones, which glistened in the light.
The cuts on his ears were covered up with plasters,
His teeth looked brand new
And now he does not haunt my bed,
He sleeps with me instead.

Julianna T (9)

Stourfield Junior School, Bournemouth

The Ganglosaur

The ganglosaur was born in a horrific geyser,
He had a muddy, rotting face covered in shells and weeds.
He breathed smoky, black fire between fangs as sharp as razors.
He plotted to steal other people's beads.

He fled his dwelling as quick as a velociraptor,
Eyes peeled for glittering, silver beads to steal.
He sprinted through caves and over mountains,
At least, he reached the town of Teel.

Once he had reached the eerie town of Teel,
He picked a fight with an unbelievably colossal African elephant.
The elephant squirted him with bewitched water
That turned his body sand-yellow,
Surely the elephants had won!

He looked down and saw his poison-green belly,
Which was as bright as the sun.

His sinfulness began to seep away
And the elephant wished the rest goodbye
By giving them a bun.

And now the geyser lies lonely and defeated,
The ganglosaur has changed too.
He has roses growing out of his golden head
And leaves flowering footprints,
Showing where he has been.

Elliott W (8)
Stourfield Junior School, Bournemouth

The Demiser

The Demiser was born in a terrific tornado,
It had grey, rough skin and ruby eyes.
It was a livid, ghastly beast
And planned other people's demise.

The monster left its residence as fast as a hawk,
Eyes peeled for helpless prey to hunt.
Speeding through towns and over mountains,
Millions heard its hungry grunts.

The Demiser finally reached the colossal beach,
Where his lightning seemed to abate him.
He saw a puddle and looked at his reflection
And saw his rough, grey skin.

The Demiser felt calm and obliging,
He was a tranquil, untroubled monster now.
The beast didn't trouble anyone either
And wasn't a cowardly cow.

He looked down and saw his hulking belly,
Which was now as blue as the sky.

His horror began to seep away
And he washed the rest goodbye.

And now the tornado lies peaceful,
With no grey, rough skin to be seen.
Instead, down towards the sea and sand,
Light-hearted footprints show where he's been.

Matilda Myers (9)
Stourfield Junior School, Bournemouth

The Creepy Creature

The creepy creature lived alone
Under a mouldy sofa surrounded by dust.
Sometimes at night, devious, demonic eyes stared,
Then spine-chilling, blood-curdling screeches could
be heard.
Fangs left blood traces on the floor
But no one had ever seen them before.

Fur was green and blood-filled as he crawled out
of his dwelling.
Out into the open, so scary indeed.
Thousands heard his bloodthirsty screams
Crawling on viciously.
Thorns like daggers, swinging wildly,
The creepy creature saw something very different
indeed.

Up above its ghastly body,
Something placid and still lay there all alone.
As he stared closer,
Water rushed around like children playing.
A very beautiful sight,
The creepy creature had never seen it before.

Starting to stare, sour, blood-filled fur,
Which was now as pale as clouds.
His creepiness turned cool and thoughtful,
No one heard a scream again.
He was replaced by a girl bunny,
She had ears as black as the night's sky.

Poppy Miller (9)
Stourfield Junior School, Bournemouth

The Flying

The Flying was born in a haunted, spooky school,
He had molten-red skin and anger running down
from his bloody eyes.
He had flaming, smoky breath
And he plotted other people's demise.

He left the school as quick as a flash,
Eyes peeled for helpless and lovely people to hunt.
Running through seas and over shipwrecks,
Everyone heard his vicious roar.

The Flying finally reached the grunting beach,
Where he got told that his dad survived the war.
Water filled his mouth like bubbly mouthwash,
It iced his cavernous throat and scorched his skin.

He stared downwards at his long arms,
Which were as pale as a piece of paper.
In a rush to find his dad,
His whole body was turning paler
And his anger began to be calm and he went to
sleep.

And now that he's found his dad,
The school lies abandoned and lonely
With no walls to be seen.
Instead, down that road,
There's a gigantic building with tiny stumps of
walls.

Alfie Joshua David Yarwood (9)
Stourfield Junior School, Bournemouth

Monster

The putrid mud monster
Lived in a deep, dark, gloomy burrow
Far below the ground
Where no bright light or fresh smell could ever
reach him.
Any time he saw his prey,
His scalp would grow up and his red, glowing eyes
would see it and pound!

As he left his dwelling,
Everyone could hear his hungry grunt
So he knew he was ready for the hunt.
The prey had no chance!

The monster finally reached the lovely park,
Where his anger seemed to fade from him.
The smell of the flowers smelt abominable to him,
He tried to dig a hole with his claws that were as
sharp as knives.
As the flaming brown cracked off his rotten skin,
He looked at his cavernous belly,
Which was now covered with a bright red jacket.

His anger began to seep away
And he washed the rest goodbye.

Now the mud-filling burrow is abandoned and
lonely.
There's no dark, muddy skin to be seen.
Instead, there are happy burrows
Showing where he has been.

Samuel Sydney Price (9)
Stourfield Junior School, Bournemouth

The Frenemy

There once was a little pile of snow,
This pile of snow grew and grew
Until it became a vicious, big snow crow.

Every freezing-cold day, it ran and ran,
Meeting other people to set gloom into their
minds.
With its knife-sharp claws and its big, black eyes,
It ran and ran until two seasons passed.

Time passed so quickly,
The snow crow saw rose-pink blossom trees
And the river roar.

He couldn't do anything,
Just wait and wait.
So he looked down at the blue drizzling river
And he saw kind, clover eyes
And a good-natured summer bird.

The cold, dark skin, the evil, black eyes
And with the power of the weather,
It transformed into some warm, light fur

And a kind, green look,
But not just that,
He became so nice!

And now the winter has to wait so long,
So long it's like he might not exist
And everybody hears the bird's lovely song,
They dance along and forget the sadness.

Aneta Banyaiova (9)
Stourfield Junior School, Bournemouth

The Stink

The Stink was born in an active volcano,
He had blood-red eyes and teeth as sharp as
fangs.
He breathed dusty smoke between very sharp
teeth
And always had a plot under his sleeve.

He left his dwelling as quick as a cheetah,
Ambushing helpless prey to attack,
Sprinting through forests and over abandoned
volcanoes.
Billions heard Stink's starving grunt!

The Stink finally reached the top of the mountain,
Where his wrath began to abate him.
A spray of snow flew from the sky like tips of
knives.
It sizzled and scorched on his molten-red skin.

He stared down at his tubby legs,
Which were now as white as soap.
His anger began to seep away
And he scrubbed the rest goodbye.

Now the vicious volcano lies abandoned and lonely
With no anger or lava-red skin to be seen.
Instead, up to the top of the mountain,
Lie tiny, happy footprints showing where Stink has been.

Sam Coltman (9)
Stourfield Junior School, Bournemouth

The Scum

There once lived a girl who dreamt bad dreams
Because there lay a scummy, rotten thing.
It had enormous, earthquaking feet
And could make people disappear.

The scum lived under a bed
As bad as could be
And never flinched
Until this day, he moved his head
And then just his lazy neck.

After lying around like an old lady,
The strange kid growled with his demonic teeth.
He went through boxes and around books
But then he found what he had never seen.

The scum slithered into the toy chest with many
toys.
His thunder seemed to abate him,
It was good to see a friend,
Even though what he was.

The scum found a peculiar thing, cuddly and centred.
It was a purple teddy, Scum looked down,
His tummy was as purple as a plum,
Like the teddy in front of him!

Now he's very kind and wouldn't hurt a fly
And cuddles the teddy each night.

Ruby Bond (9)
Stourfield Junior School, Bournemouth

The Monster

The monster lived in an abandoned car,
He had a leather black jacket with razor-sharp
spikes on his shoulders.
When he sniffed you, you could see his bright,
blood-red teeth.
He had dreadlocks down to his top lip!

He left his dwelling on a broken motorbike,
Turning corners, looking for people to pound.
Speeding through countries and abandoned lands,
Billions heard his motorbike's mighty engine.

The monster drove through the valleys and towns,
Where he was up to speed.
Until he drove into the back of a car.
So he ran, but then stopped and turned.

Then, he was a kind monster
And he was a friend to everybody.
He went down the road,
Everybody said, "Hello!"
And that is how he now lives.

And now with his old car and the darkness
With no motorbike to be seen,
But down the road is a house,
Where the jolly monster lives.

Alex Shepherd (9)

Stourfield Junior School, Bournemouth

The Grunt

The grunt lived in an abandoned, putrid dungeon
Where no one for a hundred miles could be seen.
He had decayed fangs, stolen from a sabre-
toothed tiger.
The grunt had iron-crushing hands with razor-
sharp nails.
He broke out of the putrid dungeons
Like an angry swarm of bees
Looking for terrified prey to gobble up.
This six-metre horrifying beast was all over the
news.
People panicked like a stampede.

He had finally reached the peaceful meadow
Where his killer instincts seemed to say goodbye.
The laughter hit him like strikes of thunder,
It punched and hit his monstrous hands.
He looked down at his dazzling feet,
Which were as glaring as the sun.
His frown turned upside down
And the dew washed the rest away.

And now the grunt is no grunt at all
And no killing machine
But a friend-making machine
With no anger to be seen.

Ollie (9)
Stourfield Junior School, Bournemouth

The Magma Monster

The blood-red magma monster
Lived several feet below a vicious volcano
Where he would not dare to eat a Brussels sprout
His horns stuck out of his shattering scalp
And his eyes as red as lava
And popping out of their sockets.

It left its dwelling as quick as a cheetah
Eyes peeled for tasty prey to hunt
Speeding through chaotic cities and over hills
Hundreds heard his hungry grunt.

Then one tragic, virtual day
He did the unforgettable
He ate a Brussels sprout
And then he felt a little queer.

As he approached the 'circle of life'
He looked down at his cavernous belly
And ragged, red skin had turned to lovely lime fur.

Now the volcano is as secluded as a leopard
No molten skin is to be seen

In the circle of life
There are just excited footprints
Showing where he has been.

Josh Butler (9)
Stourfield Junior School, Bournemouth

The Fiend

The fiend was born in an eerie cave,
He had blood-covered fangs and cracks in his skin.
He breathed polluted breaths through a crooked
mouth.
Every person in the world seemed to fear him.

He left his cave and bolted through town
Searching for innocent locals to eat.
Hungry and cavernous, looking for food,
He stomped the ground with his bony feet.

The fiend finally reached the beautiful village,
Where he saw a nibble of food.
He very carefully took a bite
And it completely changed his mood.

He no longer wanted to be fierce or dangerous,
He wanted to play and have fun.
His anger began to seep away
And soon, he had none.

And now the cave lies abandoned and
heartbroken,
Whilst the fiend plays with his friends.
Now all is exciting and no one is upset
And our story comes to an end.

Amelie R (9)

Stourfield Junior School, Bournemouth

The Cute Monster

The cute monster lived in a house far, far away.
He had black, smooth horns and cute, grey eyes.
He had lips as red as roses and large, round ears.

He left his habitat as cuddly as a cat,
He ran for helpless prey to hunt.
Speeding over roads and houses,
Millions heard his hungry grunt.

He finally reached the new, beautiful Co-Op,
Where people said rude things to him,
Then his well-meaning started to abate him,
His horns started growing like murder-keen knives.

He looked down and saw blood-dripping tears
from his evil eyes.
His skin turned to gravel
And his fangs were as large as water bottles,
Then he washed his kindness goodbye.

Now his lovely habitat lies abandoned and lonely
With no cute monster.

Instead, furious, bloody tears,
Showing where his sadness had been.

Calum Joyce (9)

Stourfield Junior School, Bournemouth

The Devil Monster!

The Devil monster lived under a massive, scruffy
sofa.
He had red, flaming skin and devious, horrible
eyes.
He was annoying and creepy,
He plotted people's deaths.

He left the sofa to get dinner,
He was racing through valleys and over mountains.
He was as fast as a motorbike,
Thousands heard his hungry grunt.

Finally, he got to the beach,
Then his anger went away.
The sea got him like shards of glass,
It sizzled and scorched his flaming skin,
Then he looked at himself.
He recognised something that was not himself.
He had changed.
After that, he washed the rest of his anger away.
Now the water has changed him.

Now the sofa lies abandoned and lonely
And with no red skin to be seen,
But down by the beach are happy footprints
Where he has been.

Oscar J (9)

Stourfield Junior School, Bournemouth

The Walmart Monster

The Walmart Monster was born in a volcano
And she had hot, flaming pink skin.
She had eyes as red as blood
And plotted other people's demise.

She heard the children that lived in the house
And didn't want to hear it anymore.
She was as black as the scary dark night
And had blue teeth as blue as the daytime's sky.

The door began to open,
While the children carried on playing like monkeys
having fun,
She could see the sun,
Since it was a sunny day today.

The door was wide open like a window on a hot
day so more light could come in,
It was shining on her and she changed completely.

Now she was so pretty
And the children loved her like she was their own
pet

Now the Walmart Monster lives above land
And lives with kids welcoming her.

Bethany S (9)

Stourfield Junior School, Bournemouth

The Monster

The monster lived on an abandoned island,
He had no hair and pointy ears.
He had a cat's nose and padded feet
With claws as sharp as razors.

The monster left his habitat as fast as a cheetah,
Thousands heard his extremely loud footsteps.
He carried on his journey,
Knocking over trees and climbing over hills.

Finally, he reached the blooming meadow,
Where his anger abated him.
He saw some happy kittens playing nicely,
The oldest one bit him!

Suddenly, his anger began to seep away
And his feelings changed from bad to good.
He skipped back to the abandoned island through
the forest.

Now nobody is afraid to go near him
And he finally has some friends.

Now the monster lives with friends
And they are in peace forever.

Aaliyah Samuels (9)
Stourfield Junior School, Bournemouth

Razor

Razor the monster lived deep down in a cave
Where no one could see him.
He had eyes like blood
And claws of death
And his teeth were dead sharp.
His warts were as brown as compost
And he feasted on several human limbs.

One day he left the cave to find some limbs to eat.
He flew over mountains and valleys,
Millions and millions heard his roar.

Finally, he reached a lovely, awesome garden
And took a bite of a flower.
Suddenly, he began to change,
His blood-red skin transformed to ocean-blue.
His claws turned from black to orange
And his eyes turned yellow.

And now he lives in that garden,
Watering the plants
And mowing the lawn.

So if you ever go past him,
Say hello and he'll say hi back!

Samuel White (9)

Stourfield Junior School, Bournemouth

The Joyous Beast

The joyous beast inhabited an abnormal apple,
It had spots as black as the midnight sky
And a wise, kind face,
It never made anyone cry.

It departed from its heavenly habitat as moderate
as a turtle.
Arms were ready to lift helpless prey to safety,
Over a stem and under pips,
Millions pondered the lightning speed.

The joyous beast eventually arrived
At the sight of the petrified mouse,
Where strong leg muscles seemed to vanish.
Electric swiftly flew from the cable
Like the sun gleaming,
It demolished and devoured its shell.

And now the apple resides all abandoned
With no shiny peelings to be witnessed.
Instead, slices of human flesh
And dilapidated windows,
Revealing the eerie path of the now Devil.

Fred Parsons (9)
Stourfield Junior School, Bournemouth

Ultron

Ultron lived in an old, rundown cave,
Where there was no light to be seen.
His horns as red as blood
And one metal, robotic eye,
And weeds for his hair.

He left his home for the first time in his life,
Lurking through the jungle was his prey.
As his head sweated, his eye seemed to crumple
But he didn't want to sleep
Because he would turn oh so sweet.

He had finally made it to the roaring beach,
As the sun came up, his horns began to sink slowly
into his head.
His jet-black fur began to fall off,
His hair started to turn into a colour as bright as
the sun.

Ultron now lives in a massive sand model
That he made to look like a palace.
Now there is light in every room
And he is friendly enough for you.

Aidan U (8)
Stourfield Junior School, Bournemouth

The Cambrian Psycho

The Cambrian psycho lived in an old, abandoned
building on top of a mountain,
In the middle of nowhere.
It had horrid, scaly skin,
Teeth as sharp as saws,
Eyes as red as blood
And hair as pointy as a cactus.

All of a sudden, he decided to leave his home
To see any unsuspecting victims moving around
the forest.

He sat there without one single catch in hand,
Then all of a sudden, he was zapped by a gun!
His scaly skin had turned into fluffy fur
And his teeth looked brand new
And finally, his personality had completely
changed!

Now his building is abandoned and sad,
Waiting to see its pointy hair,

Instead, cheerful drool,
Showing where he has been -
Around the bend
And straight for the end!

Travis G (8)
Stourfield Junior School, Bournemouth

The Demiser

The Demiser lived in a vicious lightning strike,
It had black, silky, crow feathers and blue, glowing eyes.
It breathed smokey breath between sharp teeth
But planned other people's demise,
Everyone said he was a devil.

It left its dwelling as quick as a swift -
Hated people and took down ships!
Killed helpless cities and villages and came to the world to hunt.
When people heard his hungry grunt,
They shut their windows and locked their doors.

The fiend finally reached the roaring beach,
Spray flew shards of water like glass
That cut his skin and absorbed the electricity on him.

He stared down at his cavernous belly and felt something.
It was fluffy, it was a puppy!
He found his heart and his true colour.

Leo Xabier Ogilvie-Arregui (9)

Stourfield Junior School, Bournemouth

The Monster

There is a little monster that lives under my bed,
His eyes are bright yellow
And his skin is blood-red.

He eats most of the chocolates that I hide under
the covers.
He only takes the caramel ones
But leaves all of the others.

One night he tried to steal again
But failed because of his nose.
As on the table, strong and clean,
Stood a beautiful red rose.

The smell filled him up right to the top
And his cloud of anger started to drop.
He looked down at the fur on his body,
Which was now as blue as the sky.
His eyes turned greener than green
And he wondered how and why.

There is a little monster that lives under my bed,
His anger has faded and his skin is no longer red.

Isabelle S (9)
Stourfield Junior School, Bournemouth

The Power Of Friendship

The monster was born in a bubbling swamp,
It had stone-like skin covered in slime
And breathed fire at a passer-by's rump,
It never took any time.

It left its dwelling with a lot of sneak,
It went over mountains and across forests,
Through oceans and valleys
But never found any people to eat.

Going over a mountain,
He encountered a little girl.
He tried to scare her
But she just gave him a pearl.

He felt his head hanging in shame,
Which was now as fluffy as a puppy.
He felt his hunger fade away
And he scared the rest away.

Now the swamp lies dried and cracked,
With no stone skin to be seen.

On the mountains now lie
Two pairs of footprints
That disappear at night.

Jack F (9)
Stourfield Junior School, Bournemouth

The Fiend

The fiend was born in a dark and gloomy cave,
He had fiery, red eyes.
He had so much hair, he had to shave
And give other people their demise.

He left his lair as quick as lightning,
Ears cupped, listening for defenceless prey.
His hungry grunt was very frightening
And he heard all the children playing.

He stumbled through the woods
And hit his head on one of the big oak trees.
He saw a blur of black hoods
But then pulled himself up with a heave.

He was delighted,
His brain had turned to the happy side.
He wasn't furious, nor sad
And his joyfulness would never hide.

And now the cave is silent,
With no monstrous growls.

Now the fiend isn't violent
And never howls.

Summer L (8)

Stourfield Junior School, Bournemouth

The Brute

The brute was created in a dilapidated cave,
It had fur as spiky as a cactus,
It hunted for animals to enslave
With a moan and a terrifying grunt in every step.

It abandoned its cave as angrily as a bear with a sore head.
Its hands ready to relieve his hunger,
Spinning through lanes and ancient forests,
After his scream, the sound would linger.

The brute finally reached the forbidden forest
Where the thunder barked as loud as a lion's roar.
Distracted, he was stung by a nettle,
Leaping back, he begged for no more.

Now the cave stands forgotten and lonely,
The brute is happy prancing around
Through the forest as if it were a catwalk,
Spreading happiness wherever he is found.

Daisy Asker (9)
Stourfield Junior School, Bournemouth

The Ogre

The ogre was established in an underwater bus,
It had spiky hair as spiky as pineapple leaves.
It hunted animals to remain fabulous,
Hair was crawling with bugs and nits.

It departed its residence as quick as a cheetah,
Stomping around, looking for delicious animals to eat.
Hunting over mountains by rivers,
Desperate to find a delightful treat.

The ogre eventually arrived at the forbidden forest,
Where the lightning seemed to taunt him.
It struck him in a ball of light,
Transforming him to a creatureless grim.

The underwater bus lies abandoned and lonely,
With no ogre to be seen.
Instead, up towards the stars and the sky
Lie radiant rainbows showing where he's been.

Lily Coltman (9)
Stourfield Junior School, Bournemouth

The Devil

The Devil lived in a mysterious chamber in the
sewers.
It had a beard as greasy as oily chips
With teeth as sharp as shark fins,
That would turn your smile upside down.

It departed from its residence feeling especially
hungry.
Its eyes gazed for animals creeping around the
smoky factories.
Rummaging through boxes and wrappers,
Its prey would not have anywhere to hide.

The Devil finally reached a creature to hunt,
He crept up with a growl in his hunger.
It got pricked by a needle poking out a wall,
It felt a tingle of a shiver.

Now the Devil has moved into a cave by the beach,
With no unhappy faces to be seen.
Making friends is what he's good at,
With no anger left.

Neve Docherty (9)
Stourfield Junior School, Bournemouth

The Ogre

The ogre was born in a cavernous dustbin,
His skin is as green as the Green Lantern's ring.
He is aggressive and vicious
And plotting other people's demise.

It left its historical dwellings as quick as Usain Bolt,
Eyes peeled for helpless prey to kill.
Sprinting over lakes and by mountains,
He wanted to kill, kill, kill!

The ogre finally reached the roaring beach,
His thunder seemed to slow down.
The blue sea touched his skin,
Making it as blue as the sky,
The thunder in him ceased to exist.

Now the dustbin is abanded and lonely
With no green skin to be seen.
His hunger and thirst completely gone,
Only happy footprints showing where he has been.

Roman Rain Hardman (9)
Stourfield Junior School, Bournemouth

The Brute

The brute inhabits in a silvery snowflake,
It is as large as a mammoth.
The snowflake fell by a nearby lake,
Exposing the brute within.

It abandoned its residents
As angry as a bear with a sore head.
Eyes peeled for vulnerable prey to devour,
Sprinting through valleys and over hilltops,
His devastating roar could turn anything sour.

The brute finally arrived at the shivering hills,
The wind began to blow him away.
An avalanche ripped through the brute,
The devil inside him began to decay.

His body shrunk as his head enlarged
And now the snowflake was nowhere to be seen.
His heart was full of kindness,
Giant snow angels showing where he has been.

Jack M (9)
Stourfield Junior School, Bournemouth

The Evil Monster

The monster was born in a ferocious forest,
Its skin was as red as blood
And it had mean, emerald eyes,
It had smelly, fiery breath and sharp teeth.

It left its dwelling as quick as a cheetah,
Looking for young people trying to be neater.
He went over hills and through rivers,
Millions heard his scary squeal.

The monster finally found a comb and a mirror
And rushed to the busy city.
He combed his hair as soft as a cushion
And his ruby-red skin turned orange.

And now the forest stands old and lonely
But the monster's all pretty
And as orange as a pumpkin
With teeth as white as snow,
As calm as a flowing river
And as happy as a rich man.

Rosemary Janet Bradford (8)
Stourfield Junior School, Bournemouth

The Devil

The Devil was born in a historic dump truck,
As wonky as a picture that had not been hung properly.
Something always stuck in his head like muck,
The Devil acted mad and peculiar.

It abandoned its abode as slowly as a snail,
Staring through the rubbish like a pack of scavenging wolves.
Always seeking a filthy rubbish trail,
Trillions heard his hungry growl.

The Devil finally arrived at the forbidden cave,
Where the evil was sucked out by a bat.
Spray flew from the bat's fangs like suncream,
There was nothing left to combat.

Now the Devil lives in a family
With his wife and children
And always smiles to everyone,
He knows everyone in town.

Bella H (9)
Stourfield Junior School, Bournemouth

The Devil

The Devil was established in a sunken shipwreck,
It had as many teeth as a ragged-toothed shark.
It roamed around causing havoc,
It was destructive and brawny and had a goatee.

It departed its abode as fast as a Formula 1 car,
Blades in hand, ready for calvary.
Ripping down trees with his tremendous muscles,
His thunder was heard all over the town.

The Devil eventually arrived at the fiend's forest,
Where his afraidness seemed to await him.
Then suddenly, his horn fell off,
Yet the Devil realised he wasn't the best.

And now he is jolly all of the time
And is skipping down the beach.
He never steals any food,
It has changed his mood.

Calum R (9)
Stourfield Junior School, Bournemouth

The Monster

The monster lived in a dark, gloomy cave,
He had yellow, mouldy teeth
And muddy, rotten skin.
He had razor-sharp claws
And eyes as red as blood.

He finally left his dangerous home
To see the outside world.
He was looking for food to hunt.

He landed in the green, new forest,
His thunder seemed to abate him.
He touched a tree and calmed even more.
He looked down at his feet,
They were as green as the forest!
His eyes were as blue as the sea,
He looked down at his cavernous belly that was
green.

And now the cave is lonely and upset,
With no monster to be seen,
But in the forest lies cheerful footprints showing
where he has been.

Ryan L (8)
Stourfield Junior School, Bournemouth

The Hack!

The mean Hack lived in a swirling swamp,
It had blood-red skin and yellow, evil eyes.
It could read minds to see what they'd done
And enjoyed blasting cities to dust.

It left its dwelling as quick as a leopard,
Looking for things to hunt or scare,
Jumping over lava pits and through mountains,
But he didn't care, he saw his destination.

The Hack went into the cavernous cave of doom
But he suddenly felt calm and all the anger was
gone.
He turned sapphire, he wondered what was
happening.
He started to walk home.

Off he went to the swirling swamp,
He joyfully skipped home,
Leaving happy footprints of where he'd been.

Joel Asher Cohn (9)
Stourfield Junior School, Bournemouth

The Beast

The beast was born in a roaring tsunami
With fur as black as the dead of night
And white, blank eyes
With yellow, wonky teeth
So people called him The Beast.

He made tsunamis every year
To make the people cry out with tears
The tsunami splashed and cried
So sadly, some did not survive.

The Beast travelled all the way to Africa
Instead of America
He saw some peckish people die
Then he felt the hole inside
And then he helped them all survive.

Now he's known as the nicest monster in the world
Because everybody spreads the word
They don't call him The Beast anymore
He's called a friend, just like all.

Ella Eva Werkentin Chant (9)
Stourfield Junior School, Bournemouth

The Devil

The Devil lived on an abandoned island,
It had ice-cold skin and one eye.
He was as slimy as a toad
With teeth as sharp as diamonds in the sky.

The Devil deserted its quarters as quick as an
elephant.
Teeth ready to dig into the juicy animals,
The animals yelped and screamed as he bit,
Screams were heard from a million miles away.

The Devil finally arrived at the stony beach,
Where his hunger started to disappear.
He stepped on the sand with his humongous feet,
The sand splashed up and sizzled on his skin.

Now his home lies with no monster to be seen,
Instead, there's lots of happy drawings
And memories in the sand.

Poppy Hannah Blair (9)
Stourfield Junior School, Bournemouth

The Brute

The brute was raised in a sunken shipwreck,
He was as long as a blue whale
With eyes as dark as a black hole
And he plotted other people's demise.

He departed his residence as quick as a Bugatti,
Arms ready for anxious prey to catch.
Frightful screams from the helpless,
It was definitely not a fair match.

The brute eventually reached the mythical forest,
He was as hungry as a horse.
A rat suddenly appeared,
The brute was bitten with an almighty force.

Now the shipwreck lies disheartened and lonely,
With no brute to be seen.
Instead, hidden among the branches,
Lie broken bones showing where he has been.

Harry Went (9)
Stourfield Junior School, Bournemouth

The Grass Block

The Grass Block was bought in a shop by a boy,
It was left forever on a shelf.
It had light green hair like bush leaves
And its only companion was a tiny, timid elf.

It deserted its shelf as rapid as a cheetah,
The Grass Block was ready to make friends.
It dodged the toys, big and small,
Thousands heard its stomping feet.

The Grass Block finally came to the bottom shelf,
When the dust entered its nasal passage.
Itching and scratching before a big sneeze,
The Grass Block transformed into the Devil.

And now the boy was older
With no toys to be seen.
Bones lay like footprints,
Showing where he's been.

Daisy Fletcher (10)
Stourfield Junior School, Bournemouth

The Shadow

The Shadow lives in a clunky dustbin,
Its hands are as sharp as a shark.
It is as hairy and scary as a yeti
And hunts its prey with a growling bark.

It deserts its quarters as quick as a cheetah,
It hunts night and day
Hands ready to pounce and consume
Screams can be heard from a million miles away.

The Shadow finally reaches the amazing beach
Where the clouds surround it
Water flies like diamonds in the sky
It moans and groans from the pain on its skin.

And now the dustbin lies happy and abandoned
With skin as blue as the sky
Instead in the sand and the sea
Lie footprints leading to the ocean.

Millie Fisher-Wyatt (9)
Stourfield Junior School, Bournemouth

The Orb!

The orb was born in a vicious, terrifying wave
He was a mean, wild and fuming creature
With a red and yellow fiery body.

No friends, all alone, poor Orb
Oh, oh, oh!
No one liked him, no, no, no
He had long, wide feet, oh.

The waves were as big as an elephant
Evil, red colours is all he can see.

One day there was a storm
And the orb was electrocuted
Then all of a sudden
The orb became good and calm.

He moved on to a new blue house
Now the orb is a pleasant, level-headed
And soft-hearted creature
Now he has lots of friends
Yes, yes, yes!
Everyone likes the orb in his home.

Evie Millington (9)
Stourfield Junior School, Bournemouth

The Imp

The imp was born in a storming tsunami,
It had a tail like a plank of wood.
It had eyes as black as the night
And spied on people trying to hide.

It left its habitat as quick as a gleam of sunlight,
Tail ready for helpless prey to slap.
Jumping over trees and under bridges,
Thousands could hear his hunger snap.

The imp arrived at the obscene volcano,
Where his anger seemed to abate him.
The view changed him
And he washed the rest goodbye.

And now the tsunami lies abandoned and lonely,
With no watery skin to be seen.
Instead, down towards the town,
There are lovely smiles all around.

Iris F (8)
Stourfield Junior School, Bournemouth

The Blood Demon

At the bottom of the deepest, darkest cave
Lived a demon in the day.
Where no life could live,
He had horns as sharp as knives
With blood dripping from one.
At night, he went to hunt for men.

One terrifying night he went out for his
bloodthirsty hunt.
To his horror, a dazzling light in the sky.
He started shrinking and got lighter,
He began to shrink and shrink
Until he was as small as a football.

Now there's no one who is to be devoured
Or killed by the blood demon
And now he has a new name, Rainbow Dude,
And now the cave is abandoned
With no blood demons left.

Logan William Goodfellow-Martin (9)
Stourfield Junior School, Bournemouth

The Devil

The Devil was born in a crooked house
And it had rotten, old teeth.
It breathed disgusting breath from its teeth,
It killed other people's lives.

It left its home as quick as a flash
And it had glowing eyes that were good for
hunting.
Fists ready to kill,
Thousands could hear his angry grunt.

The Devil finally reached the beautiful beach,
Where he ate a delicious banana.
As he swallowed, he felt a tingle all over
And hit his head with a faint.

The house lies lonely and sad
With no Devil to be seen.
The Devil is no longer mad,
He skips across the beach.

Troy Wilson (9)
Stourfield Junior School, Bournemouth

The Gonk

The Gonk was born in a vicious thunderstorm
With glowing, white skin and black, beady eyes.
It breathed lightning breath
And plotted other people's demise.

It left its home as quick as a swift,
Speeding through valleys and over mountains,
Thousands could hear its hungry grunt.

The angry Gonk finally reached the roaring beach,
Where his anger seemed to abate him.
Spray flew from the sea like strips of bacon,
It sizzled on his lightning skin.

He stared downwards at his glowing feet,
Waiting in the storm.
The calm Gonk smiled,
Then turned into a magic cloud.

Joe Nash (9)
Stourfield Junior School, Bournemouth

The Monster

This monster was never seen
But it's obvious where he has been.
Only when the moon is bright
Will he appear on a starry night.

Born in a lava pit,
Dark and fiery
And very well lit.
Like a ball of burning heat,
He rolled away on his own two feet.

He was looking for mayhem to watch
But his evil just went down a notch.
He saw all the people play
So he ended up going there every day.

Now he's a good fellow
And no more blazing eyes of yellow.
Now at the age of eighty-three,
He's sat on his chair drinking his favourite -
Iced tea!

Harry Illsley (9)
Stourfield Junior School, Bournemouth

The Monster

The monster was born when a lightning storm struck.
He had redder skin than the Devil
And old, but very new, clothes.

He would try to kill and would always succeed,
He would laugh with cheer and a cheeky grin
As he walked through slaughtered villages.

A snowstorm hit...

Frozen ice drops surrounded him,
His cheeky grin suddenly lost,
His smiled turned down.
Ice drops made a flash
And he started to smile again
But he didn't want to kill anymore.

Now the lightning monster is calm and happy
Because he now knows he did the right thing.

Keira-Anne Erwood (9)
Stourfield Junior School, Bournemouth

The Zoocha

The Zoocha was born in a zoological zoo,
It had ruby-red, flaming skin and pitch-black eyes.
It blew out rage with its mean, dagger teeth,
The Zoocha was plotting demise.

It flew out of its dwelling as sharp as an eagle,
Looking for things to destroy.
Speeding through valleys and over mountains,
Hundreds heard his low pitch name.

The Zoocha saw a beautiful stag,
His heart started to lift.
His skin turned blue,
He got the gift of evolving into Zachoo.

His skin now sapphire,
Eyes bright emerald,
Rage and anger locked up inside.

Oliver Knighton (9)
Stourfield Junior School, Bournemouth

The Slenderman

The monster was born - negative lightning,
He was like a devil and really liked fighting
With white skin, glowing, yellow eyes
And a heart full of sin.

He lifted his hut as quick as a flash,
Eyes peeled for a village to smash.
Speeding through streets, he went to the beach,
Thousands heard his ear-cracking screech.

After years of travelling,
He finally reached the golden, sandy, roaring
beach.

He stared downwards and saw his cavernous belly,
Which was now as calm as a rainbow,
Smelling like flowers,
And he washed the rest goodbye.

Matthew Dewerenda (9)
Stourfield Junior School, Bournemouth

The Spalpeen

The Spalpeen inhabited a deep, starless hole,
He stood as tall as an oak tree.
He smiled brightly through his shining teeth
And filled others with glee.

It began to depart from its hole,
Finally seeing the sun.
The Spalpeen dashed into the street,
Ready to have some fun.

He finally found an ice cream van,
Where he decided to try some,
But it drove away too quickly
And left nothing for the young.

Now his hole is empty,
No happiness to be seen.
The Spalpeen has become angry
And very, very mean.

Finley Stephen Smithers (9)
Stourfield Junior School, Bournemouth

The Ivysaurus

On the side of a mountain
In a deep, dark hole
Lived an ivysaurus
As dirty as a mole.

Spiky, dry and thorny
Rotting and wilted
Ivy clung to his green, crumbled skin
Then his journey suddenly stilted.

The lake overflowed
Water gushing, away he went
Waves rushing.

Drowned and wet through
He finally stopped
Opening his eyes
He gazed at a beautiful, new world.

He drank and stretched,
Looking up to the sun.
Luscious green leaves glistened,
His real beauty for all to see.

Evan Stoddart-Ceren (9)
Stourfield Junior School, Bournemouth

Space Beast

The space beast lived on a fire-blasting planet,
He lived under a volcano.
He had eyes as bright as the sun
And toes as long as trees.

His fangs were as sharp as knives,
He had breath as gross as a skunk
And eyes as red as blood.
He left his planet as quick as a ship,
The space beast shot through Neptune,
The planet he was looking for was not there.
He was confused!
Finally, the space beast saw it,
The planet he was looking for -
Planet Earth.
The space beast saw the happy people
And turned good.

Tom C (8)
Stourfield Junior School, Bournemouth

The Tutu

The Tutu was born in an ancient, wonderful
waterfall.
It had big, bulging thorns and ruby, fiery eyes
With teeth as sharp as a blade.
Tutu liked crushing homes and people.

It left home as quietly as a rat,
It ran as fast as a cheetah.
It was rushing to mountains and rivers,
It heard a scary squeal.

Tutu finally found a person and crushed her and
her home.
It felt happier and turned light brown,
It felt loved like a baby.
Its heart felt like it was wrapped with love
And its teeth turned as white as milk.

Louise Aravell Calimlim Manabat (8)
Stourfield Junior School, Bournemouth

The Friendly Whale

In the gloomy clouds
There was a strange sound
Some with a kiss and a roar
It was a meteor
He crawled out as quick as a bird on the hunt.

He looked for prey
While ripping up a village
Suddenly, he saw himself in a mirror
His skin turned aqua blue just like the ocean
Hands turned into fins, legs were now a tail
But he is a big whale.

Now he lives under the waves
Where people never age
The moon stays bright
Just pale white
Rocks create underwater caves
He is generous.

Lola Bea Whitney (9)
Stourfield Junior School, Bournemouth

The Revenger

The Revenger was born on a calm wave
But he never respected his home.
One day the wave put him in a cave,
He called the coast guard on his phone.

Soon the coast guard arrived,
The Revenger took the boat and disappeared,
He strived and strived until he got to a village.

He tried to persecute the villagers,
He also wanted to eat
So he found an ice cream van,
Which was no mean feat.

Suddenly, a rock fell on him,
From that day on,
He stopped his infuriating roam.

Archie Arthur Hamilton (9)
Stourfield Junior School, Bournemouth

The Fiend

The fiend was born in a rainy rainforest,
It had leafy, green legs and red, glowing eyes,
It blew a mean roar and liked killing people.

It left its dwelling as quick as a diving peregrine falcon.
Piercing eyes looked for a tribe to eat,
Lots heard his electrocution,
Glass breaking and scratching.

The fiend finally found a tribe of twenty people,
"Don't worry, I'm vegetarian," said the fiend.
With a happy smile, he turned happy
With a blue mouth and tiny feet.

Ewan Brooks (9)
Stourfield Junior School, Bournemouth

The Monstrous Monster

The monstrous monster, born in a calm wave,
Was mean and fluid like jelly.
He wobbled his big, fat belly,
He had a head like a bear.

The monstrous monster had a temper like a goblin,
He always flipped like a pyre.
His eyes like a goblet of fire,
He looked with his eyes and began to calm.

The monstrous monster went to the beach,
At that moment, a strike of thunder hit!
He changed because he was electrocuted,
He sat and felt the anger wash away.

Charlie Jones (9)
Stourfield Junior School, Bournemouth

The Bad Thing

The bad thing was bad and mad,
He liked to be rigid and sad.
He was born in thunder
And zoomed through the valleys and over
mountains.

The bad thing was frightening like lightning
And went to a beach and saw himself in the
sparkly blue sea.
He looked up at the stars and realised why he was
mean.

He stared downwards and saw his belly,
Which was now as blue as a nice, calm sky.
His anger began to seep away
And he washed the rest goodbye.

Sammy Soltys (9)
Stourfield Junior School, Bournemouth

The Monstrous Monster

The monster was born in a humongous wave,
He was as fierce as a lion and as unkind as a
shark.
He enjoyed hunting people after dark.

One time, while he was crashing and thrashing,
He caught sight of himself in a mirror.
He looked at himself and saw flaming blue eyes,
Suddenly he realised what others despised.

After that, no one saw the humongous beast
again.
Instead, in its place, was a miniature, friendly
wave.

William Adams (9)
Stourfield Junior School, Bournemouth

Shadow Storm

The shadow storm was born in a vicious tempest
And he's never to be seen.
If you touch him, you'll be dead for the rest of your
life!
He is grey and blue with a silvery ear.

As he walked, he felt calm and kind,
Maybe he could be your friend?
Watch if he turns blue and black,
He could suddenly turn back!

Harry Kenyon (9)
Stourfield Junior School, Bournemouth

My Greatest Fear

Sent from Hell to bring Hell to Earth
Deliberately hunts in the middle of the night
Just because of pure spite.

He's a snake-like, misery monster
But instantaneous death is his speciality
He's a mad, midnight murderer
With bloodstains all over his body.

The tentacles that wrap about his neck
With one touch, the enemies are stunned
But his main lethal weapon is indeed his tongue
Because one touch, one feel, one taste, equals
death!

His usual midnight phrase is always -
"Feed me your blood and bones!"
Which is why we named him Blood and Bones.

Paddy Hazeldine (10)
West Monkton CE Primary School, Taunton

The Kid Next Door

I peeped through my fence this morning
And nearly fainted at the sight.
Jimmy, the kid next door,
Had grown curly horns overnight!
As I followed him to school,
I saw him waggling a tail.
He even paused and bent to eat,
a raw, fat, slimy snail!

As he thumped into class,
Nobody seemed to care
That poor Jimmy Jones had grown green clumps of
hair!

Lunchtime was quite disturbing,
I spied Jimmy at the rubbish,
Devouring up the leftovers,
Cold chips and festering fish.
I offered him a sandwich,
A small bite of my 'Angel cake',
He gobbled up my entire lunch
With fangs as sharp as a rake!

In football, Jimmy popped the ball with his
enormous claws.
By the time we left our school today,
He was walking on all fours!

In my bed I lay awake, too terrified to sleep,
Listening to poor Jimmy Jones wail and whine and
weep.
Like a wolf I hear him howl a spine-chilling sound,
In the shadows of his garden,
He paces round and round.
There is something though, that I fear more,
My own discovery.
There is now a monster in my mirror,
Staring back at me!

Reece Fortnum (9)
West Monkton CE Primary School, Taunton

Zeigblab The Great!

Zeigblab was born in a bottle of Coke
The thing it will poke
Will turn into smoke
It turned to brown
Then it went down
Now he lives on sand
But he plays in a band
He goes to Nando's
But only eats monsters
He plays Fortnite
But he gets a fright
When he gets sniped
He gets hyped
Now he's grown twelve toes
There's no point going to Nando's
As he has one finger on his hand
So he couldn't play in the band
Now he plays Fortnite with his feet!

Lewis Ward (10)
West Monkton CE Primary School, Taunton

The Monster's Tea

The monster of the city, fierce and bold,
The monster whose feet are dipped in gold.
His breakfast, his dinner and even his tea,
All glisten brightly like the stars in the blue sea.
He eats and munches until the day is done,
For the monster is giant and scares everyone.
He wakes at the crack of dawn
And instantly, the city dies.
No one leaves while they're under his rule,
No one dares go near him as he roars and roars!
But the sad truth is, he is just lonely and bored.

Jacob Stone (10)
West Monkton CE Primary School, Taunton

Riley The Monster

My monster is called Riley,
He is very smiley.
We are best friends
And he comes round every weekend.

He has three round, googly eyes
That makes a puddle when he cries.
Beautiful fur like a rainbow
That the wind could blow.
His legs are very hairy
But it doesn't put off his wife Mary.

Riley is very funny,
Everyone laughs till it hurts their tummy.
Everybody is cheerful when he is around,
He is the funniest guy in his hometown.

Isabella Pereira (10)
West Monkton CE Primary School, Taunton

My Monster

My monster has one eye
My monster never dies
My monster is emerald green
My monster is super keen
I love my monster.

My monster is a king
My monster wears a diamond ring
My monster is a food lover
My monster has not got a mother
I love my monster.

My monster likes to clap
My monster likes to trap
My monster likes to take naps
My monster loves me
My monster knows I love him.

Imogen Canney (10)
West Monkton CE Primary School, Taunton

Bow

Bow, the dragon unicorn
Who likes to wear her bows
Red, green, purple and pink
Are her favourite colours
When she pulls her bows on
She sings and dances and hollers.

Bow's best friend is Laser Beam Betty
When she comes around Bow's for tea
She likes to bring lots and lots of spaghetti.

Bow loves her bows so bright and sparkly
She has a collection as high as a pineapple tree.

Grace Olivia Baker (10)
West Monkton CE Primary School, Taunton

Monster-Candy-Corn

He is as striking as lightning
But he's not very frightening.
With his candy-coloured fur
And his soft, gentle purr.

He has a cape and a horn,
Which he calls a corn.
After, he had a very pleasant encounter with a
unicorn.

His rainbow-coloured hair gives him such flair
As he shows off his magic tricks
At the midnight monster fair.
Come and see him if you dare!

Josie Leanne Corry (9)
West Monkton CE Primary School, Taunton

Big Red And Me

Big Red sat on my bed, sitting next to me
He came to me from the Himalayas
For some tasty tea
It was a long and tiresome journey
That made him sing a song
That was as long as long can be
And went on and on and on!
His fur was like sheepskin
His claws sharp like knives
They stood out like shining pearls
Drifting along the sea.

Cameron Gage (10)
West Monkton CE Primary School, Taunton

The Monster

The monster had wings like two surfboards
And fangs like knives
A head like a little chunk of comet
Body like a mini, strong man
Nails and toenails like claws
He was born with undead souls
And horns made of bones
From the victims he'd killed
All he wants is them to see him as a picture
At least a picture of something niceish!

Luke Christopher John Rees (10)
West Monkton CE Primary School, Taunton

The Red Monster

Once there lived a red, one-eyed monster,
He wandered the streets alone
With fuzzy hair and he was stinky,
All he could do was moan.

Longing for some friends to play with
So he could have some fun,
But everyone he met was scared of him.
No matter how hard he tried,
He couldn't be friends with anyone
And he was young.

Kaden Stretton (10)
West Monkton CE Primary School, Taunton

Ocean Creature

Very deep in the big seas
Lived a monster who liked the ocean trees.
He was big and blue
And his fur was like glue.
He kept lying every day
And his favourite month was May.
When he saw a frog,
He started barking like a dog.
He was as good as bad,
But even more mad.
He had a prawn as a friend
So this is the end!

Zuzanna Bukowska (10)
West Monkton CE Primary School, Taunton

The Monster Called Bob

There was a monster called Bob
Who was part of a mob
He was so tall
He owned a mall
And dreamed of owning a pool.

The pool would be so big
It would take years and years to dig
A hot tub or two would have to do
A big house and a car
Maybe a mouse and a bar.

Theo Bimson (10)
West Monkton CE Primary School, Taunton

186

Mysterious Monsters

(Haiku poetry)

A grr and a roar
And a delicious galore
Monsters cheering more.

Are you friendly or
As scary as you can be?
None of you scare me.

A monster monster
How do you know who he is?
He could be sweetness.

Antennae-shaker
Lots of minds filled with wonder
A fluffy hugger.

Rosina Coppola (10)
West Monkton CE Primary School, Taunton

Barry Bogey Claws

Barry Bogey Claws
Listens to no laws.
I am from Planet Cuna
And they told me to go.
He walks on buildings, cars and motorbikes,
So you know he is not afraid of heights.
He scratches you with a big claw
And it is as sharp as a shark's jaw.

Mason James Kew (9)
West Monkton CE Primary School, Taunton

The Gentle Monster

He was tall like a giant
He was hairy like a bear
He had five eyes but didn't care
His feet were very big
His claws were very sharp
He was a smelly monster
Because he loved to fart!

Ruby Wyatt (10)
West Monkton CE Primary School, Taunton

Monster Poem

(Haiku poetry)

Monsters, scary, large,
Eyes like a fireball glowing,
Chasing kids in dreams.

Monsters, cute, tiny,
Eyes like fluffy unicorns,
Dancing on rainbows.

Carys Griffiths-Jones (9)
West Monkton CE Primary School, Taunton

The Monster

(A kennings poem)

Creepy crawler
Powerful biter
Super scarer
Sneaky sneaker
Smart thinker
Terror creator
Children hater
Mayhem causer
Nightmare maker.

James Metcalfe (10)

West Monkton CE Primary School, Taunton

Good Monster

(A kennings poem)

Bow wearer
Cuddle lover
Mud hater
Friend maker
Jewellery maker
Dress lover
Forest hater
Lemonade maker
Good monster.

Kadie Hollins (10)
West Monkton CE Primary School, Taunton

Bogey Monster

Bogey-green monster
Slimy and gooey, *achoo!*
Hide or he'll get you
And cover you in goo!

Kobi Loveridge (10)
West Monkton CE Primary School, Taunton

YOUNG WRITERS INFORMATION

We hope you have enjoyed reading this book – and that you will continue to in the coming years.

If you're a young writer who enjoys reading and creative writing, or the parent of an enthusiastic poet or story writer, do visit our website **www.youngwriters.co.uk**. Here you will find free competitions, workshops and games, as well as recommended reads, a poetry glossary and our blog.

If you would like to order further copies of this book, or any of our other titles, then please give us a call or visit **www.youngwriters.co.uk**.

Young Writers
Remus House
Coltsfoot Drive
Peterborough
PE2 9BF
(01733) 890066
info@youngwriters.co.uk